For my father, Harry S. London
LCDR U.S. Navy, Ret.
1915-1995
and for my sons, Aaron & Sean

Printed in the United States of America
First Edition   1 2 3 4 5 6 7 8 9 10
Library of Congress Cataloging in Publication Data
London, Jonathan.
Old salt, young salt / by Jonathan London; illustrations
by Todd L.W. Doney.
     p.   cm.
Summary: Aaron's dad is an experienced sailor, and
Aaron must find his sea legs when they go out together
for a day of fishing on the bay.
ISBN 0-688-12975-7. — ISBN 0-688-12976-5 (lib. bdg.)
[1. Boats and boating—Fiction.
2. Fathers and sons—Fiction.
3. Fishing—Fiction.] I. Doney, Todd,
ill. II. Title.
PZ7.L8432Ol 1995
[E]—dc20 94-14593 CIP AC

OLD
SALT
YOUNG
SALT

by Jonathan London
illustrations by Todd L. W. Doney

LOTHROP, LEE & SHEPARD BOOKS
NEW YORK

It was our day to go out to sea together—just Dad and me. Bodega Bay was foggy, but it was a bright fog, as if the sun was hiding just behind, ready to show its face.

Dad asked some men nearby to help carry our boat down to the water.

"I can help," I said, joining the men.

"Watch out!" Dad shouted, and they almost plowed me down.

When the boat was bobbing in the foam, I splashed into the water and climbed aboard. Dad soon had the outboard motor attached, and the men shoved us off.

We puttered to the mouth of the bay and bumped over the sea. The gulls circling overhead cried a sad, sad song.

"What's the matter, Aaron?" Dad asked. He was back in the stern, holding the tiller. I was up in the bow. The sun was burning a hole in the fog. "C'mon, Aaron," he said. "What's the matter?"

"I'm big enough to help carry a boat, Dad."

"Well, mate," he said, "when you find your sea legs, I'll let you run the motor. How about that?"

"What are sea legs?"

"That's what Old Salts like me call it when you can walk on a boat or a ship at sea and not fall down," said the Old Salt, who was once an officer in the navy. "And not get seasick, either," he added, looking a little green himself.

"I feel fine," I said. "See, I can walk—"

"No! No!" Dad shouted. "Sit down!"

Dad gunned the motor and we were off and flying, me hanging on in the bow. The boat slammed over the waves, which were growing bigger and bigger.

"Yee-*haw*," I cried. "Ride 'em, cowboy! Bucking bronco!"

That's when I saw it. A spout!

"Dad, look'it!" I pointed. Dad slowed down. He was really green now. His head was hanging over the side.

Then I saw the most amazing thing I've ever seen. A *whale!* It rose clear out of the water and practically danced on its tail. It was as big as a school bus. Water streamed off it, and a big eye looked down at me. Then the whale crashed over with a huge kaa-*plash,* and Dad and I were both drenched.

"Gray whale," mumbled my Dad. "They're migrating north for the summer."

He leaned over the side and threw up—"*Blah!*"

I held my nose and giggled and said, "Dad, maybe I should steer now. Okay?"

"Well . . . ," he said, wiping his mouth with his sleeve. A puff of wind swept toward us, ruffling the waves like corduroy. "It's a bit rough for that. Here." He handed me his rod. "You can do the fishing. We'll troll for salmon. I'll head over into the lee of that island, where it's calm."

Seals barked on the rocks, and the waves smoothed out where the island blocked the wind off the sea. Dad cut the motor and showed me how to let the line out behind the boat and set the drag for trolling. "If a salmon strikes," he said, "hang on tight. I'll come help."

We sliced through the sea at trolling speed, slow, and I gripped the pole, waiting for a fish to strike. I waited and waited and waited. It was hot. My clothes had dried, and I felt like jumping overboard, or out of my skin. Dad hummed the same old tune over and over. It sounded like the drone of the motor.

Suddenly the pole jerked in my hands and bent almost double. "Dad!" I shouted. "I got one!" I tugged with all my might, the reel hissing and clicking like Dad's ten-speed bike.

"Hold on!" Dad yelled, cutting the motor. He came toward me. The boat lurched on a wave and he tripped and fell. "Oooh! My nose." Blood oozed between his fingers.

The rod was alive in my hands, shaking and bouncing. A big, silver fish flashed near the boat and danced on its tail, just like the whale.

"Loosen the drag!" Dad hollered through his nose—which he was holding with his old red bandanna.

"I don't know *how!*" I hollered back.

"Then let go of the rod! The line will snap, or the fish will pull you in!" But I didn't. I held that rod tight, and I started winding in the line. It was hard work. The handle of the reel kept slipping, and the line zinged out of the spool.

The big fish dived down deep.

The pole stopped bending. The reel stopped spinning. The line stopped tugging, as if there was nothing at the other end.

I was about to give up when the fish jumped three times and the rod almost flew out of my hands. I reeled in fast, bracing my feet. I yanked hard on the pole. My dad reached for the fish with his net and missed. But then it slapped smack into the bottom of the boat, where it flipped and flopped.

"I *did* it!" I shouted. "All by myself."

"A chinook!" said Dad. "A *salmon!*"

Dad held the fish up. "Your first salmon," he said with a huge grin. The fish was as long as my arm. It still flapped like mad, flashing silver and green in the sun.

Dad strung the salmon on a stringer and let it drag over the side in the water. "Supper tonight," he said. "And *you* are going to clean it. I'll show you how."

"*Now* can I steer the boat?" I asked, as proud as a fisherman can be.

"Well . . . okay, mate. If you can come aft without falling down."

I headed back, stepping carefully over the seats and tackle.

"Stay low," Dad said, "and hold on to the gunwales." The boat rolled and pitched up and down with the sea.

"You made it!" he said. "Here's the tiller. Now keep the prow aimed toward Bodega Head." He pointed toward the tall cliffs, which looked as thin as a pencil in the distance. He showed me how to twist the handle to speed up or slow down.

Dad crawled forward, still holding his nose, still green in the gills, then sat and watched me proudly as I steered the boat all the way back to shore.

When we landed on the beach, Dad let me help carry the boat out of the water with the other men. It was weird, though; now the land seemed to roll like the waves.

That night, when Dad came to tuck me in, he said, "You had quite a day today, Aaron. You saw your first whale, caught your first salmon, and handled the boat like a real seaman."

"I guess I found my sea legs. Right, Dad?"

"Aye," he said with a chuckle. "Now good night, mate." He stood tall and saluted. "Salty dreams."

My bed rolled like our boat and rocked me to
sleep like the sea.
And all night long, I was the captain of my dreams.